Désirée Hirst MA B.Litt, Oxon

Brodie's Notes on

T. S. Eliot's Selected Poems

Pan Books London and Sydney

KU-357-239

First published 1980 by Pan Books Ltd
Cavaye Place, London SW10 9PG
　3 4 5 6 7 8 9
© Désirée Hirst 1980
ISBN 0 330 50175 5
Filmset in Great Britain by
Northumberland Press Ltd, Gateshead, Tyne and Wear
Printed and bound by
Richard Clay (The Chaucer Press) Ltd, Bungay, Suffolk

This book is sold subject to the condition that it
shall not, by way of trade or otherwise, be lent, re-sold,
hired out, or otherwise circulated without the publisher's prior
consent in any form of binding or cover other than that in which
it is published and without a similar condition including this
condition being imposed on the subsequent purchaser

Contents

Page and line references in these Notes are to
the Faber paperback edition of *T. S. Eliot: Selected Poems*,
but as the poems are separately analysed, in alphabetical order,
the Notes may be used with any edition of the poems

To the student

A close reading of the text is the student's primary task.
These notes will help to increase your understanding and
appreciation of Eliot's poetry, and to stimulate *your own* thinking
about it: *they are in no way intended as a substitute* for a
thorough knowledge of the poems.

The poet and his work

Thomas Stearns Eliot (1888–1965), an American who became a naturalized British citizen, was one of the most original and influential 20th-century poets writing in English. He helped to change the whole nature of poetry – its style, its content. A shy retiring person, he was averse to investigation into his life, though many studies now exist.

Eliot was born in St Louis, Missouri, in the United States, where his grandfather the Reverend William Greenleaf Eliot was a Unitarian minister. His grandmother Abby Cranch was the daughter of a district judge from Washington. His father Henry Eliot became a St Louis businessman and married Charlotte Stearns, a schoolteacher from New England. The poet was their sixth and youngest child. The family spent their holidays near Gloucester in Massachusetts, where Henry Eliot had brought some land.

In 1905 Eliot entered Harvard University, where he later developed an interest in philosophy, especially the work of the English philosopher F. H. Bradley, and where he took courses in Comparative Religion – studying in particular Hinduism and Buddhism and learning some Sanskrit, though concentrating on the European classics. In 1910 he went to Paris, where he studied the work of the French symbolist poets – Jules Laforgue and Baudelaire in particular – after which he returned to Harvard. About this time his friend, the poet Conrad Aiken, relates that Eliot frequented a well-known gymnasium in Boston where he met the original of Sweeney Todd. Finally, to complete his studies he went to Merton College, Oxford in 1914. He felt uncomfortable in wartime Oxford; in 1915, after he had met and married Vivien Haigh-Wood, the daughter of a portrait painter – and aided by a small allowance from his father – he took a post teaching in High Wycombe Grammar School.

In the autumn of that year the Eliots moved to London, where he taught at Highgate Junior School, all the time experimenting in writing poetry. During World War I he was part of the intellectual group gathered round Lady Ottoline Morrell, and the Eliots became very friendly with the Cambridge philosopher Bertrand Russell (1872–1970).

By 1916 Eliot's thesis on Bradley was finished and was despatched to Harvard and accepted. He was, however, unable to cross the Atlantic in wartime to take his doctorate formally; he never actually received the degree.

In 1917, through a friend of the Haigh-Woods, Eliot was offered a post in the Colonial and Foreign Department of Lloyd's Bank in the City, which he kept until he moved into the publishing firm of Faber and Faber (then Faber and Gwyer) in 1926. His friend and mentor Ezra Pound (1885–1972), the American poet and impresario of literature, saw to it that when the English writer Richard Aldington (1892–1962) gave up the post of assistant editor to Harriet Weaver (editor of the experimental journal *The Egotist*), Eliot was appointed in his place. In 1919 Leonard and Virginia Woolf (1880–1969 and 1882–1941) published T. S. Eliot's *Poems* from their new Hogarth Press, while Harriet Weaver turned *The Egotist* into a publishing firm, bringing out *The Love Song of Alfred J. Prufrock*.

Eliot now began to review for *The Times Literary Supplement*, and during this time conducted Extra-Mural University Classes on the Elizabethan and Jacobean poets and dramatists. Another collection of poems entitled *Ara Vos Prec* came out in London with John Rodker, and the New York firm of Knopf brought out *Poems by T. S. Eliot*. Also published in London was Eliot's book of collected essays, *The Sacred Wood*, which appeared in 1922.

In 1921 Eliot published an appreciation of the music of the Russian composer Igor Stravinsky (1852–1971), in the 'London Letter' of the American Journal, the *Dial*. He had been greatly impressed by Stravinsky's ballet *Le Sacré du Printemps* ('The Rite of Spring') – 1913 – in which the famous Russian dancer Vaslav Nijinsky (1890–1950) danced, Eliot became a lifelong friend of Stravinsky.

In November 1921 Eliot was given leave by the bank to go to Lausanne to take a rest-cure under Dr Vittoz; while there he wrote *The Waste Land*. The following January, passing through Paris on his way back to London, he handed the manuscript to Ezra Pound. It was published in the *Dial* and in the *Criterion* (which Eliot founded, and edited 1922–39). Then, with the help of John Quinn, the Irish-American patron of letters (to whom Eliot donated the manuscript), *The Waste Land* was published in book form in both London and New York.

In 1925 Eliot published *The Hollow Men*; after joining Faber's as an editor he wrote the *Ariel Poems*, then *Ash Wednesday* (dedicated to his wife), and *Marina*, published in 1930.

In 1927 he was formally received into the Anglican Church, having been brought up a Unitarian. Throughout this time his wife Vivien was becoming increasingly mentally disturbed, having also suffered physical ill-health. In 1932 Eliot paid a visit to America; on his return he sent solicitor's letters to Vivien, making it clear that he was separating from her, though he would continue to support her financially. They met only once more before her death in 1947.

Meanwhile Eliot was working on his series of poems *Four Quartets*, published together for the first time in 1944. He had also begun his career as a dramatist with his choruses for *The Rock, a Pageant Play* (1934) and *Murder in the Cathedral* (1935), to be followed by *Family Reunion* (1939) and *The Cocktail Party* (1950).– through the influence of the Anglican dramatic producer E. Martin Browne.

In 1948 Eliot received the Nobel Prize for Literature and moved into the home in Cheyne Walk, Chelsea, of his friend, the critic John Hayward. Eliot's late plays *The Confidential Clerk* (1950) and *The Elder Statesman* (1956) followed. His close relationship with his secretary at Faber's, Valerie Fletcher, led to his second marriage in 1957.

T. S. Eliot turned his personal and professional difficulties to magnificent creative account; after a mellow and honoured old age he died in January 1965, one of the major Christian poets of the twentieth century.

Further reading

Four Quartets, T. S. Eliot (Faber)

The Art of T. S. Eliot, Gardner, Dame Helen (Faber)

T. S. Eliot's Poetry and Plays, Smith, Grover (Univ. of Chicago Press)

T. S. Eliot's 'Waste Land', Williams, Helen (E. Arnold)

The Quest of the Holy Grail, Weston, Jessie (Frank Cass) – (her *From Ritual to Romance* is unfortunately out of print at present)

Yeats, the Tarot and the Golden Dawn, Raine, Kathleen (Dolmen Press)

Twenty-two Keys of the Tarot, Ussher, Arland (Dolmen Press)

Style and influences

As a poet Eliot was seriously attempting to hammer out a new type of English verse. He was in reaction from the subjective emotional intensity of Romantic Poetry and impatient with the pastoral sentimentality of the succeeding Georgian style. ('Georgian' covers the poetry most widely popular in the early years of George V's reign; often concerned with country life. Edward Thomas in this country and Robert Frost in America could be called Georgian poets; another 'Georgian', Rupert Brooke, was particularly popular.) Dame Helen Gardner who has studied Eliot's poetic form in her *Art of T. S. Eliot* (Faber) – the allusions here are to the 1968 edition – describes 'the characteristic metre of "Prufrock" as "an irregularly rhyming verse paragraph in duple rising rhythm" – that is in feet of two syllables with the stress on the second; what is often called by the name of the Latin foot, the "iamb".' The rhyme pattern is decorative, not regular and 'there is, beside the variety in the amount of stresses in the line, considerable variety in the amount of coincidence between speech stress and metrical stress'. She points to the use of a similar form by John Donne and George Herbert, and in Milton's *Lycidas*, 'On Time', and 'At a Solemn Musick'. Certainly Eliot had become fascinated by 17th-century verse, and particularly by metaphysical poetry, when preparing Extra-Mural classes. And his influence was to promote a revival of interest in the work of a group of poets who had been underestimated. In 'La Figlia Che Piange' the metrical stress comes most often on the first syllable of each foot, however, and Dame Helen describes 'Mr Apollinax' as 'a poem built upon a conversational phrase: a piece of free accentual verse'.

Blank verse of the very free kind used by the later Elizabethan and Jacobean dramatists who so much interested Eliot – Middleton, Tourneur, Webster, Ford and Marston – is used for the 1920 poems. The verse stresses and the pauses within the line are placed with great variety and there is an 'absence of the strong beat which the coincidence of speech and metrical stress give'. The verse mode of these dramatists is used again with great skill in *The Waste Land*, where there are pointed echoes from their plays and from Shakespeare. But the opening lines return to the pattern of 'La Figlia

Che Piange' with its falling rhythm, or trochees: the stress on the first syllable of each foot. And the pub scene in 'A Game of Chess' is entirely colloquial. Later, starting in *Ash Wednesday*, Eliot began experimenting with the four-stress metre he developed fully in the *Four Quartets*.

The year Eliot spent in Paris, from 1910–11, brought him into contact with recent French poetry; the influence of Rimbaud, Baudelaire and Jules Laforgue was strong in his earlier work. He always remained deeply devoted to the great Catholic Florentine poet of the Middle Ages, Dante Alighieri (1265–1321) and was particularly haunted by passages from the *Purgatorio* out of Dante's epic *The Divine Comedy*, where the poet is conducted first by his predecessor Virgil through the state of Hell and later by his beloved Beatrice through those of Purgatory and Paradise. But perhaps the most immediate poetic influence on Eliot came from his American friend Ezra Pound, whose role as an impresario and editor was even more impressive than his success as the author of *The Cantos*. (Another influential American poet friend was Conrad Aiken.) Well grounded in Latin, less so in Greek, Pound was attracted to exotic languages like Chinese or Provençal. Possibly Eliot's preoccupation with Arnaut Daniel (the Provençal poet who addresses Dante in the *Purgatorio* in his own tongue) and his message, may have been the effect of Pound's enthusiasm. Pound, through his contacts, did a great deal to promote the publication of Eliot's work and as the editor of *The Waste Land*, he reduced a brilliant but undeveloped mass of verse to the form we know and admire.

But for some years Eliot had concentrated more on philosophy than on literature; his own thesis for Harvard University, for which he also researched at Merton College, Oxford, was on the English philosopher, F. H. Bradley. The tentative nature of many of Eliot's poetic statements echo Bradley's scepticism and his disbelief in the value of abstruse thought trained upon precise ends. At Harvard, too, Eliot had followed courses on Hindu and Buddhist thought, so naturally phrases from Buddha's 'Fire Sermon' and *The Upanishads*, or early Hindu dialogues between sages and disciples, find a place in *The Waste Land*. But equally the influence of a 1916 bestseller, *My Past*, by Countess Marie Larisch (niece of the Austrian Empress Elizabeth who was assassinated while boarding a steamer on Lac Leman, cousin of the Archduke Rudolph and of Ludwig of Bavaria who met his death by drowning), has left its trace, as George L. K. Morris pointed out in *Partisan Review*, March 1954. (Her home was on the Starnberger-See and she had a notable encounter with Richard Wagner.)

Finally, the devotional influence of High Anglicanism affects all Eliot's later work. Brought up a Unitarian, he was received into the Anglican Church at Finstock parish church in June 1927. The work of the Anglo-Catholic scholar Evelyn Underhill on Christian mysticism particularly coloured Eliot's thinking; not unexpectedly, we find echoes from the poem of St John of the Cross, for example. Among other scholarly works, Eliot drew upon Jessie L. Weston's study of the pre-Christian elements in the Arthurian legend, *From Ritual to Romance*, Jackson Knight's studies of Virgil, and his friend Charles Williams's preoccupations with Magic, Myth and Theology, especially his knowledge of the Tarot Cards.

Poem summaries and textual notes

The Ariel Poems

These poems were written and published between 1927 and 1930. Faber published the *Ariel Poems* in a series by contemporary writers. They reflect Eliot's commitment to the Church of England – he was confirmed in 1927 – and to his naturalization as a British subject.

Journey of the Magi

This poem forms an expression of Eliot's final conversion to Anglicanism. He admits being impelled towards this decision in part at least by his reaction to Bertrand Russell's *A Free Man's Worship* (*Time*, 6 March 1950). The Magi are making a journey between two worlds; between BC and AD, two world ages. Their feelings are naturally ones of disorientation; and the romance and excitement of their quest, as described in Matthew, 2,1–2, is deliberately deflated by Eliot's treatment of the event. His poem expresses exhaustion and disillusion, but also the triumph of faith.

There is an obvious drawing upon Lancelot Andrewes (see note below). Echoes from Pound's 'Exile's Letter' also appear; and from *Anabase* by the French symbolist poet St John Perse – an account of desert exploration that Eliot had been translating since 1926.

the Magi Wise men from the East, who have seen from their astrological calculations that the Messiah, or King of the Jews, has been born.

A cold coming ... very dead of winter Eliot has here 'lifted' – almost word-for-word – a part of the famous 17th-century sermon preached by Lancelot Andrewes in the presence of King James I of England.

a tavern with vine-leaves ... pieces of silver ... empty wine-skins These lines portray vividly one of the disillusioning episodes on the Magi's journey. The 'dicing for pieces of silver' suggests a prediction of the Roman soldiers' drawing of lots for Christ's garments; and of Judas Iscariot's betrayal of Christ for 'thirty pieces of silver' (Matthew, 25,15).

This Birth ... bitter agony ... like Death Eliot was to repeat this theme in Part 3, lines 131–2 of 'East Coker' (1940), the second poem in his *Four Quartets* (1944): 'the agony/Of death and birth'.

no longer at ease ... another death The Magus now speaks of his own feelings on returning to his Kingdom: after the Birth he can no longer feel at ease in his country, or with the old religion. He wishes for 'another death', presumably his own. (He is possibly echoing Eliot's own disillusionment with contemporary life.)

A Song for Simeon

Based on the prayer 'Nunc Dimittis': 'Lord, now lettest thou thy servant depart in peace' (Luke, 2,29–32), spoken by the ancient temple priest Simeon, this poem expresses, again, a sense of suspension between two worlds and a longing for personal death. But there is far more looking towards the future in Simeon's version than in that of the Magi. Both the passion of Christ and the destruction of Jerusalem are anticipated.

Like a feather ... hand Perhaps an echo from *King Lear*, V,3,261–7 – 'I know when one is dead ... This feather stirs – when what is probably Cordelia's 'death-rattle' gives Lear temporary hope that she still lives.

And a sword ... thine also This is a quotation from Simeon's words to the Virgin Mary (Luke, 2,35), 'Yea, a sword shall pierce through thine own soul also.'

Animula

This is the study of a child, a 'simple soul' just issued 'from the hand of God', with a child's joy in simple things. But, faced with the 'pain of living and the drug of dreams', the child 'issues from the hand of time ... selfish, misshapen, lame'. The language of the poem is obliquely sensual (lines 3–7), as a young child is innocently sensual. And there is a despairing cynicism in the last line, 'Pray for us now and at the hour of our birth.'

Animula The title derives from Hadrian's evocation of his soul (translated by Byron), with Eliot taking as his starting point lines from Dante's *Purgatorio* 16:
From the hand of Him who loves her before she is, there issues, in the manner of a little child that plays, now weeping, now laughing, who knows nothing save that, moved by a joyous creator, she turns willingly to that which gave her pleasure ...

Encyclopaedia Britannica The authoritative English encyclopedia, in several volumes. The word 'Encyclopedia' means 'instruction in the whole circle of learning'; the first edition was published, in successive numbers, in Scotland in 1768–71. There have been many editions since then, and the Encyclopedia is constantly revised.

Guiterriez ... Boudin These names are apparently entirely fictional, though Boudin seems to have been derived from the Emmaeus episode in James Joyce's *Ulysses*.

Floret This name, though also fictional, carries overtones of the myth of Adonis, beloved of Venus, who was killed by a wild boar; or that of Actaeon the hunter who was turned into a deer by Diana and torn to pieces by his own hounds; or of Dante's greyhound Velto.

Pray for us now ... our birth An inversion of the words of the Roman Catholic 'Hail Mary': 'Pray for us sinners now and at the hour of our death.'

Marina

The character of Marina is taken from Shakespeare's *Pericles*. She is the lost king's daughter who has to be sought over the seas. The recognition scene, Act V, Scene 1, is invoked – especially as a contrast to Hercules's recognition of his terrible situation when he wakes to discover he has killed his own children in his rage of madness.

The link with the sea is important and in his first draft Eliot mentions a particular stretch of known coastline; where Rogue Island lies off Caxo Bay in New Maine at the mouth of New Meadow River. The daughter in this poem, again in some ways reminiscent of Shakespeare's Cordelia in *King Lear*, presents an aspect of Eliot's 'Hyacinth Girl', more positive than her appearance in *The Waste Land*. A reconciliation and movement towards a higher state, as in Dante's portrayal of the relations between himself and Beatrice, are continually suggested.

Quis hic locus ... mundi plaga The epigraph is taken from *Hercules Furens*, line 1138, by Lucius 'the Younger' Seneca (*c*.5 BC–AD 65). Hercules, awakening from a spell of madness, is asking, 'What place is this, what land, what quarter of the globe?' – a style echoed in the first stanza of *Marina*.

woodthrush Eliot could mean either the ordinary thrush or the missel thrush, a larger and less musical bird that feeds mainly on mistletoe berries. Both have brown backs and wings, with lighter, spotted bellies, and belong to the *Turdidae*, the family that also includes nightingales, blackbirds etc.

bowsprit A strong spar projecting over a ship's bows, and to which are attached the forestays that support the foremast.

garboard strake The first range of planks laid on a ship's bottom, next to the keel.

caulking Sealing (a ship's) seams with waterproof material.

Ash Wednesday

Part 1

The opening lines echo Guido Cavalcanti's poem '*Perch' io non spero di torner giammai*' ('Because I do not hope ever to turn again'). The ballad was translated by Daniel Gabriel Rossetti (1828–82) under the title 'Ballata, Written in Exile at Sarzana'. The fact that the Lady in Tuscany, to whom Cavalcanti wishes news of his illness to be conveyed, is most probably his wife, also has special relevance to Eliot's poem. *Ash Wednesday* is in a special way written for his first wife Vivien; in a sense it represented both a farewell to her – for her increasing instability meant he felt he had to separate from her – and also a tribute to Vivien as his Muse. And the French poet Charles Baudelaire (1821–67) caught Eliot's attention (noted in his *Essays Ancient and Modern*, 1936) with his letter to Mme Marie: 'Through you, Marie, I shall be strong and great like Petrarch, I shall immortalize my Laura. Be my guardian Angel, my Muse, and my Madonna, and lead me in the path of beauty.'

The basic message of Part 1 is a prayer for God's forgiveness for the poet's past transgressions. Lines 32–3 ('For what is done ... upon us) perhaps echo Psalm 130,1–5 in the Anglican Authorized Version of the Bible. And the section ends with the words from the Roman Catholic 'Hail Mary': 'Pray for us sinners now and at the hour of our death.'

to turn again During this period of his life Eliot was turning more and more towards the Anglo-Catholic movement in the Church of England, so it is natural that phrases from the Anglican liturgy for Lent should re-echo through the poem; the refrain of 'to turn' echoes words from the prophet Joel, 2,12: 'Therefore also now, saith the Lord, turn ye even to me.'

this man's gift and that man's scope These words are an obvious echo of Shakespeare's Sonnet 29, line 6: 'Desiring this man's art, and that man's scope'.

aged eagle stretch its wings The image of the 'aged eagle' is taken from the bestiary fables, which show the eagle in old age flying upwards towards the sun; then, plunging into a well, it is rejuvenated. There is also reference to Canto 10 of Dante's *Purgatorio*: Ganymede raised by the eagle to the sun. There is also the ironic fact that Eliot sometimes signed himself 'Apteryx' ('Wingless').

vanished power ... usual reign Wordsworth's *Immortality Ode* seems to have contributed to this phase.

wings are no longer wings to fly This has echoes of Lancelot Andrewes's Ash Wednesday sermon of 1602: 'What then, shall I continually fall and never rise? Turn away and not once turn again? ... Shall these swallows fly over up and put me in mind of thy return ... ?'

Part 2

This section represents an Annunciation sequence, but this time the salutation comes from the Lady as it does in Dante's *Vita Nuova*, 3: 'This wondrous Lady appeared to me clothed in whitest hue ... and of her ineffable courtesy, which now is rewarded in the world above, saluted me with such virtue that I thought then to see all bounds of blessedness.'

Three white leopards ... bones ... already dry In the first seven lines there is an association with the Valley of the Dry Bones in Ezekiel 37,1–14. The Lady will make the dry bones live – which the three leopards have picked clean. This spiritual death, of heart, liver and brains, is also symbolized (as Leonard Unger has pointed out) by Grimm's fairy story *The Juniper Tree*.

the strings of my eyes Signifying the bond of love with the Lady, who by her withdrawal impels the speaker towards his necessary spiritual death. The words are taken from John Donne's love poem 'The Extasy'.

Rose of memory ... is now the Garden The rose symbol used in these lines is a love symbol, encompassing both the dedicated love of the Virgin, the 'Mystical Rose' (taken up by Dante in his *Paradiso*) and that of the Courtly Love tradition, as exemplified by *The Romance of the Rose* (*Roman de la Rose*, begun *c*.1240 by Guillaume de Lorris, completed forty years later by Jean de Meung: the first part is romantic; the second, by de Meung, realistic and cynical).

the bones sang They were 'chirping/With the burden of the grasshopper' (lines 64–5 above) – Ecclesiastes, 12,5: 'and the grasshopper shall be a burden, and desire shall fail'. The speaker in the poem has undergone the necessary death which the quester in *The Waste Land* was so reluctant to undertake. (Of course, the 'burden' of a song also relates to its words and message.)

This is the land ... divide by lot   The section ends with another reference to Ezekiel (Chapter 42): 'This is the land which ye shall divide by lot unto the tribes of Israel.'

Part 3

This section uses the image of the Winding Stair, perhaps inspired by Dante's climbing of the Mount of Purgatory. Temptations assail the speaker at the turn of each stair. A window over the third stair looks out over an alluring landscape: a pastoral scene. Part 3 ends with words from the prayer of the centurion in Matthew, 8,8: 'Lord I am not worthy ... but speak the word only ...'

second stair ... of hope and of despair   The first stanza sets the scene: there are overtones from Rossetti's 'Love's Nocturne': 'Ah! might I, by thy good grace/Groping in the windy stair ... Meeting mine own image there,/Face to face.'

Damp, jagged ... aged shark   These brilliantly descriptive lines contain references to a text from St Paul on 'putting off the old man' (Ephesians, 4,22), and to Shakespeare's *Macbeth*, Act IV: 'maw and gulf/Of the ravin'd salt-sea shark'.

slotted window bellied like the fig's fruit   Another striking simile, but here extremely sensual.

Blown hair ... over the mouth ... Lilac ... hair   Conrad Aiken's *The Charnel Rose*, 1922, uses the image: 'Bright hair, tumbled in sunlight ... they are no longer sweet'. In the sensuality of 'Lilac and brown hair' (line 113) there are reminiscences of the lilacs and 'the smell of hyacinths' in Eliot's 'Portrait of a Lady'. (Shades of purple, violet, lilac recur throughout Eliot's poetry; and hyacinths are said to have been his favourite flowers.)

Part 4

The words of Arnaut Daniel in the *Purgatorio* are recalled. Matilda is evoked from Canto 28: 'who went singing and plucking flower after flower, wherewith her path was pied'. The different feminine figures in this Part are run together: St Lucy, Dante's guide through Purgatory, Matilda and the Virgin herself are all suggested. In line 145 the speaker uses a text from St Paul, in which Paul exhorts the heavens to 'redeem the time, because the days are evil'; and the past is reclaimed and sanctified.

the violet and the violet A colour that, as we have noted, seems to have had a special significance for Eliot. It figured in the cult of the god Attis, representing both death and the irresistible life force.

Sovegna vos Daniel Arnaut's Provençal version of the French imperative, '*Souvenez-vous*': 'Remember'.

The years that walk between The middle years of life.

jewelled unicorns ... gilded hearse This image poses a problem: some critics, such as Grover Smith, consider it sinister, comparing it to the procession of Lucifera and her gaudy train of vices in Spenser's *Faerie Queene*, Book 1; and to Blake's 'Marriage hearse' from his lyric 'London' in *Songs of Experience*. Others like George Williamson see the unicorn as belonging to the legend of the Virgin. According to other Medieval legends the unicorn often represents Christ himself, and is shown as drawing the Ark of the Covenant – the holy emblem of the Law in the Old Testament.

silent sister veiled ... yews ... garden god ... flute The silent veiled sister is connected with the symbol of the yew, emblem of both death and immortality; the breathless flute of the garden god, also connected with the Attis cult, clearly has sexual connotations.

fountain sprang up ... bird sang These symbols are pointers towards Hope.

wind ... thousand whispers The wind is the breath of the Spirit.

Part 5

'In the beginning was the Word, and the Word was with God, God, and the Word was God ... And the light shineth in darkness; and the darkness comprehended it not.' (John, 1,1–5). Part 5 is a prayer to 'the veiled sister', the Virgin Mary, to pray for mankind that has lost the Word, and 'walk in darkness'. For the Word is still there: 'And the light shone in darkness ... the unstilled world still whirled/About the centre of the silent Word.'

O my people This refrain throughout the section comes from a part of the liturgy for Good Friday, and is derived from the prophet Micah's lines in Chapter 6, verse 3 of his exhortation: 'O my people, what have I done unto thee?'

No place of grace The lack of true peace – 'the Peace that passeth understanding' – is the reason for the block in the unfolding of grace.

those who ... are terrified and cannot surrender   Their need is for
  surrender to the word, but they are frightened and obstinate.

The desert in the garden ... withered apple-seed   There are
  overtones from another prophet, Joel, 1,12: 'the pomegranate tree, the
  palm tree also, and the apple tree, even all the trees of the field, are
  withered: because joy is withered away from the sons of men.'

Part 6

Echoes of Guido Cavalcanti and Baudelaire run through this final
section. The repetition of the expression 'sister' recalls Baudelaire's
line, 'Mon enfant, ma soeur' ('My child, my sister') from his poem
'L'Invitation au voyage'. The 'Lady' of Part 2 and the 'sister' of
Parts 4 and 5 are here the 'blessed sister, holy Mother' – all, of
course, the Virgin. Indeed (as in an orchestral symphony), Eliot
brings together in Part 6 themes from earlier sections; for example:
the 'I do not hope to turn again' and the 'wings' (here 'unbroken')
of Part 1; the 'garden' of Parts 2 and 4; the 'desert' (here 'sandy
earth') of Parts 2 and 5; the 'lilac' of Part 3; the 'yews' of Part
4; the 'blue rocks' of Part 5. (This is a device often employed by
Eliot – for example, in the famous first and last lines of 'East Coker'
in *Four Quartets*: 'In my beginning is my end ... In my end is my
beginning' – Parts 1 and 5.)

And the blind eye creates   There are overtones here from Dante's
  Purgatorio, in the concept of God's will on 'that sea to which all moves
  that it createth and that nature maketh'.

Our peace in His Will   Further overtones of Dante, from the *Paradiso*,
  3,86, in the prayer for peace, 'whose service is perfect freedom'. (See
  also preceding textual note on Part 5, 'No place of grace'.)

Suffer me not to be separated   From the ancient Latin hymn, the
  'Anima Christi' ('Soul of Christ') used in the Roman Catholic Church.

And let my cry come unto Thee   The final line of the section, and of
  the poem, comes from Psalm 102: 'Hear my prayer, O Lord, and let my
  cry come unto thee.'

Choruses from 'The Rock'

These choruses were designed for a production by E. Martin
Browne for the Forty-five Churches Fund in 1934. They represent

Eliot's first attempt to return to drama after *Sweeney Agonistes*. Eliot's task was simply to fill in Martin Browne's framework, but he took the opportunity to introduce passages from the sermons of Hugh Latimer, the English Protestant martyr (*c*.1485–1555): 'The Sermon of the Plough' and 'Second Sermon Preached before the Convocation of the Clergy'. There are overtones from Kiplingesque comic songs in the Workmen's chants, as Grover Smith points out. And there is clearly a borrowing from Shakespeare's use of the poet Gower, in his Romance Play *Pericles*, in the treatment of the chorus.

In general, the choruses express the atmosphere of the depression of the thirties, with their evocation of the hunger marches, strikes and falling stock markets. The approach in 'The Rock' is one of straightforward moralism (e.g. lines 1–37), rather than the more mystical tone of the *Four Quartets*. Eliot's work on the choruses did, however, help to arouse again his interest in drama, and so led to his writing *Murder in the Cathedral* and, later, *Family Reunion*. Finally, it must be admitted that the emphasis at the end of Chorus 7 on Usury, associated with Lust and Power, is uncomfortably reminiscent of Ezra Pound's preoccupation with the subject.

the Rock The title refers to the Christian Church – 'thou art Peter [*Petra*: 'rock'], and upon this Rock I will build my church' (Matthew, 16,18).

Chorus 1

The Eagle soars ... Hunter with his dogs The constellations of the Eagle and Orion the hunter prefigure the changing seasons. And there are anticipations of the *Four Quartets* in the first five lines of this Chorus.

the Word Again 'the Word' reverberates throughout the Choruses. (See summary of *Ash Wednesday*, Part 5.)

Hindhead or Maidenhead The first is in Surrey, the second on the Thames in Berkshire; both are attractive spots for a Sunday-morning's visit.

***Enter the* ROCK, *led by a* BOY** The little child leading the personified Rock is a biblical echo from Isaiah, 11,6: 'the leopard shall lie down with the lamb ... and a little child shall lead them'.

desert ... tube-train next to you Again Eliot uses the symbol of the desert; here he specifies that the desert is within us. (Tube-trains operate in London's Underground railway system.)

no man has hired us One of the biblical echoes in the Choruses; see
Matthew, 20,7: 'because no man hath hired us'.

a shortened bed ... a narrow sheet The chant of the Workmen,
answering the unemployed, gives an optimistic forecast, denying the
prophecy of Isaiah 28,20: 'For the bed is shorter than that a man can
stretch himself on it; and the covering narrower than that he can wrap
himself in it.'

Chorus 2

Spirit ... waters ... lantern ... tortoise The end of line 7 refers to
Genesis 1,2: 'And the Spirit of God moved upon the face of the waters';
then the 'lantern set on the back of a tortoise' is an allusion to
traditional Eastern imagery, where in the Creation myth the world is
seen as balanced on the shell of a tortoise.

love our neighbour A reference to the words of Jesus to the young
man, in Matthew, 20,19: 'Thou shalt love thy neighbour as thyself.'
(The words also appear in Leviticus 19,18.)

Whipsnade A large 'open' zoo (cages are used as little as possible) in
Bedfordshire.

dash to and fro ... casual pillions There are echoes from *The Waste
Land* here, in the emphasis on futile frivolity. The telling and
memorable line, 'And daughters ride away on casual pillions', would
indicate a 'generation gap' then too – perhaps it always exists, for all
generations!

race reports These refer to the horse-racing news in the papers –
nothing to do with ethnic minorities.

land of lobelias and tennis flannels This refers to prosperous
suburbia, e.g. the 'stockbroker belt' in Surrey or Sussex, within
commuting distance of London.

cavies ... marmots American rodents, especially the guinea-pig ...
burrowing rodents.

the Stranger 'The Stranger', in lines 53–76 is of course Christ.

Chorus 7

In the beginning ... the deep Another reference to Genesis 1,1–2.

withered ancient look ... child ... starvation A moving description,
one with which we are today tragically familiar through reports of
starving children in the Third World.

Then came ... moment in time ... gave the meaning Lines 18–20
refer, of course, to the birth, life and crucifixion of Christ.

Chorus 9

Joyful communion of saints Words from the Apostles' Creed in the
Christian Church: 'I believe in . . . the Communion of Saints'.

Chorus 10

great snake The Devil.
put out the light and relight it Probably echoes here of Genesis 1,3–5:
'And God said, Let there be light; and there was light . . . And God
called the light Day, and the darkness he called Night.' Possibly also an
optimistic reversal of Othello's lines in Act II, Scene 1: 'Put out the
light, and then put out the light.'

The Hollow Men

In this almost unrelievedly depressing poem Eliot is saying that
we are all 'hollow men', with stuffed bodies, straw-filled heads.
The atmosphere is one of aridity, cacti, stone images. There are
references to Shakespeare's *Julius Caesar*, Dante's *Divina Commedia*
(the *Inferno* and *Paradiso* sections) and Conrad's *Heart of Darkness*;
also to Guy Fawkes and scarecrows.

Mistah Kurtz—he dead From *Heart of Darkness* by Joseph Conrad
(1857–1924): the black servant is giving the news of the death of the
European, Kurtz, who, treated as God in the Congo, was described as a
'hollow sham'.
The Hollow Men The title has overtones of *The Hollow Land* of William
Morris (1834–96) – the influential English craftsman, poet and prose-
writer; *The Broken Men* of Rudyard Kipling (1865–1936); and
Shakespeare's *Julius Caesar*, IV,2,23–7:

But hollow men, like horses hot at hand,
Make gallant show and promise of their mettle;
But when they should endure the bloody spur,
They fall their crests, and, like deceitful jades,
Sink in the trial.

A penny for the old guy Folk rhyme celebrating Guy Fawkes' Day
(5 November).

Part 1

stuffed men ... filled with straw ... dry cellar Another reference to
Guy Fawkes: his stuffed effigy, and the fact that he hid, with the
gunpowder, in the cellars of the Houses of Parliament.

Those who have crossed ... death's other Kingdom Overtones of Charon, ferryman of the dead who, like the 'old guy', exacts payment.

Part 2

Eyes I dare not meet in dreams Dante: *Inferno*, Canto 3; *Paradiso*, Cantos 31–2. Eyes are seen in both a sinister and a sublime light in the poem.

wear ... deliberate disguises ... field ... wind behaves Lines 31–5 carry overtones of the straw-stuffed scarecrows farmers erect in their fields to scare birds away.

Part 3

stone images Refers to the idols of pagan religion: e.g. the 'standing stones' and dolmens of Europe; the giant stone heads of Easter Island in the Pacific.

Lips that would kiss form prayers A reference to 'Art' from *The City of Dreadful Night and Other Poems* by James Thomson (1834–82): 'Lips only sing when they cannot kiss.'

Part 4

There are no eyes here ... hollow valley ... Multifoliate rose The 'eyes' again. Echoes of Dante's *Inferno*, 3, lines 79 and 97–9: 'Abashed I dropped my eyes'; and 'of that sour/Infernal ferryman [see 'Charon' in note on 'Those who have crossed', Part 1 above] of the livid wash,/Only his flame-ringed eyeballs rolled a-glower'. The 'Multifoliate (many-leaved) rose' refers to the hope that may be found from the eyes in the *Paradiso* that lead to the Mystical Rose [the Virgin, but also Dante's Beatrice].

Part 5

Here we go round the prickly pear An echo of the children's-games song: 'Round the Mulberry Bush' and 'Gathering Nuts in May'. The prickly pair belongs to the *Opuntia*, a genus of cactus growing in arid regions of North and South America.

Between the idea ... Falls the Shadow These three stanzas (lines 72–90) have their source in the famous poem to Cynara by Ernest Dowson (1867–1900), 'Non sum qualis eram' ('I am not now as I once was'), with its refrain, 'I have been faithful to thee, Cynara, in my fashion': there the 'shadow' is the shadow of Cynara.

For thine is the Kingdom The ending of The Lord's Prayer in the Anglican Church: 'For thine is the Kingdom, the Power and the Glory, for ever and ever. Amen.'

the way the world ends ... a whimper One of Eliot's most quoted lines. Its sad cynicism appealed to the hopeless-helpless feelings of the politically aware before World War II. (Though today, in our fears of a final nuclear explosion, the 'big bang' seems more liable to be 'the way the world ends'.)

Poems 1920

Gerontion

The first lines are from A. C. Benson's biography, *Edward Fitzgerald* (1905): '... in a dry month, old and blind, being read to by a country boy, longing for rain'. Possibly 'hot gates' is an allusion to the battle of Thermopylae (480 BC). The speaker describes the Jewish owner of his house in terms borrowed from the Elizabethan and Jacobean dramatists: for example, Tourneur (*The Revenger's Tragedy* 3,4); Middleton (*The Changeling* 5,3); Chapman (*Charles Duke of Byron* 5,3 and *Bussy D'Ambois* 5,4); and Ben Jonson (*The Alchemist* 2,3 and 3,2). There are two Shakespearean references: *Antony and Cleopatra* 2,2 and *The Merchant of Venice* 2,1.

Again, there is a theory of memory derived from Henri Bergson, whose *Creative Evolution* (1937) defines duration as 'the continuous progress of the past which gnaws into the future and which swells as it advances.'

The literary biographer and critic Grover Smith suggests there are also evocations of James Joyce's *Ulysses* with its hero Leopold Bloom. T. S. Eliot admired this great novel and tried to persuade Leonard and Virginia Woolf to publish it with their new firm, the Hogarth Press. However, Eliot's treatment of the Jewish figure is sarcastic, in contrast to Joyce's.

The unease caused by the state of despair in the poem is increased by the presence of the Spring season, a time of year always particularly disturbing to Eliot. 'April is the cruellest month' is the opening line of *The Waste Land*. There is also a correspondence, as Grover Smith suggests, between 'Gerontion' and the Fisher King (uncle of Perceval in the Grail legend, and who figures in many other myths and legends), used symbolically in *The Waste Land*, where he waits in a state of inertia for salvation. The theme of 'Gerontion' certainly anticipates *The Waste Land* in many ways.

Gerontion The poem's title suggests the hero of the poem by the theologian Cardinal Newman (1801–90), 'The Dream of Gerontius', where an aged man meeting death is represented.

Thou hast ... dreaming of both This is a quotation from Shakespeare's *Measure for Measure*, III,1,32–4.

merd Turds, excrement.

Swaddled with darkness An echo of Matthew 12, quoted in *Seventeen Sermons on the Nativity* written by Lancelot Andrewes (1555–1626): '... rolls it about with swaddling bonds of darkness'.

juvescence Youth.

Christ the tiger Perhaps from William Blake's lyric 'The Tyger', or possibly an allusion to Henry James's 'The Beast in the Jungle'.

May, dogwood and chestnut The source here is *The Education of Henry Adams* (History of the United States of America, Ed. Ernest Samuels). Adams took chaos to be the normal state, order to be the 'dream of Man'.

Vacant shuttles/Weave the wind See Job 7,6–7.

Concitation An excitation.

These with a thousand ... mirrors An echo of *The Alchemist* by Ben Jonson (1572–1637).

whirled ... fractured atoms This uses the 'limbo' concept found in *Paradise Lost*, Book 2 and Chaucer's *Parlement of Foules*, 80. There are suggestions of 'unnatural vices' in the state of despair Eliot is describing.

driven by the Trades An indication that the speaker has been a sailor in his time.

Burbank with a Baedeker: Bleistein with a Cigar

The dawn in Venice conjures up the vision of Cleopatra's barge at Cydnus, this time bearing the Princess Volupine. By contrast the Jew Bleistein lifts his gaze to a work in perspective of the artist Canaletto (1697–1768), but lowers it with thoughts of the Rialto, the Venetian exchange, raising shades of Shylock from *The Merchant of Venice*. The piles on which Venice stands are undermined by rats, but the Jew is underneath it all. (Here Eliot shares the unfortunate anti-semitism of his friend Ezra Pound.) The merchant prince Sir Ferdinand Klein – with overtones from *The Tempest* – entertains the Princess Volupine. She has the air of a decadent, consumptive voluptuary. Meanwhile Burbank speculates on who clipped the mane and claws of the Lion of St Mark in Venice – reminiscent of Shakespeare's sonnet, 'Devouring Time, blunt thou the lion's paws'. He invokes Ruskin's laws of growth and decay as set out in *The Seven Lamps of Architecture* (1849) and *The Stones of Venice* (1851–3), philosophizing on the passage of Time, which has earlier been symbolized by a candle burning down – possibly the emblematic candle in the Mantegna painting.

Tra-la-la-la-la-la-laire From a song of Théophile Gautier (1811–72), 'Sur les Lagunes' (*Variations sur le Carnavale de Venise*).

nil nisi divinum stabile est The motto from a candle in a painting of St Sebastian by Andrea Mantegna (1431–1506): 'Nothing is permanent unless Divine; the rest is smoke.'

the gondola ... grey and pink From Henry James's *The Aspern Papers*: 'The gondola stopped, the old palace was there ... "How charming! It's gray and pink!"' This gives the link with the Venice sequence in *Othello* 4, 2.

goats ... hair too An echo of Browning's *Toccata of Guluppi's*, also associated with Venice: 'Dear dead women, with such hair, too – what's become of all the gold/Used to hang and brush their bosoms? I feel chilly and grown old.'

so the countess passed The final direction from the Jacobean dramatist John Marston's masque, *Entertainment of Alice, Dowager Countess of Derby*.

Niobe The classical mother figure who in Greek legend (Homer's version) boasted of her six sons and six daughters to the goddess Leto, whose only children were Apollo and Artemis. Enraged, Leto sent Apollo and Artemis to kill Niobe's children. Weeping, Niobe was finally turned into a stone on Mount Sipylus, which still drips tears.

They were together A modified line from Tennyson's 'The Sisters': 'They were together and she fell'.

Defunctive Connected with death, funereal.

the God Hercules A reference to Antony and Cleopatra 4,3, where the God Hercules, Antony's patron, is heard leaving him to strains of unearthly music.

protozoic slime Slime containing protozoa, the most elementary form of life.

Sweeney Erect

Apart from more criminal associations (T. P. Prest's *Demon Barber of Fleet Street* who used to convert his customers into meat pies), 'Sweeney' is the name of a legendary Irish King who was changed into a bird. Here he sets off hysterical reactions through the more sordid connection with Edgar Allen Poe's *Murders in the Rue Morgue*, where the murders are triggered off when a pet orang outang steals his master's razor and starts to shave his face with it. The incident from *The Odyssey* is also evoked, where Odysseus startles the bathing Princess Nausicaa by his sudden appearance from the bushes; Sweeney is compared to the uncouth giant Polyphemus.

The epileptic fit of the woman on the bed, provoked by Sweeney's testing his razor, is coped with by Doris bringing sal volatile and brandy. The ape-like shadow of Sweeney, 'addressed full-length to shave', dominates the scene and forms a parody of Emerson's definition of history as 'the shadow of Man'.

Cyclades Greek islands.
anfractuous A geological formation of broken rocks.
Aeolus The god of winds; here the rising, or 'insurgent', winds.
Ariadne The daughter of King Minos of Crete, deserted by Theseus who had carried her off from Crete. She had helped him to find his way through the labyrinth by means of a ball of string, and so to succeed in his task of slaying the Minotaur. From Ovid's *Heroides*.

A Cooking Egg

Dated 1919, the title of this poem refers to the kind of egg that is not quite fresh but which can still be used for cooking. The speaker sees himself as such an object.

In the first scene the heroine Pipit receives the speaker in her own setting. The third scene is set in an ABC (Aerated Bread Company) café, a place where the poor, including the 'red-eyed scavenger' [possibly dustmen], echoed from Villon, can afford to eat. The sequence, according to Grover Smith, is of a grown man's visit to a childhood sweetheart: later he is sitting in a café, reflecting on how time has divided them – just as he has earlier speculated on the next life.

En l'an trentiesme ... hontes j'ay beues The epigraph, in 15th-century French, is from the opening lines of *Grand Testament* by François

Villon, the 'vagabond' French poet (1431–?): 'In the thirtieth year of my age,/When I have drunk all my shame.'

Pipit The girl's name conjures up the impression of a small charming bird-like creature.

Daguerreotype An early type of photograph on a glass plate. In the second section the speaker thinks of what he may look forward to in heaven, by contrast. There he could have the sensational figure of Lucretia Borgia, the Renaissance daughter of the notorious Borgia family of Popes and poisoners, for his bride. He could have as his guide the famous 19th-century Russian Theosophist, Madame Blavatsky, or Piccarda de Donati, one of Dante's guides in the *Paradiso*.

the penny world The egg and what it symbolizes.

The Hippopotamus

Clearly inspired by the contemporary French poet, Théophile Gautier's 'L'Hippopotame' in his *Poésies Diverses*; the poem was written in 1917.

The Epigraph is from the letter of the early Church father, St Ignatius, to the Trallians (with references to the Church of Laodicea in St Paul's Epistle to the Collossians 4,16 and to Revelation, 3,14–18) where St Ignatius exhorts reverence for bishops, priests and deacons who are the support of the Church itself.

The poem is, in fact, a defence of the ordinary lukewarm practising Church member.

hippopotamus An echo of Lewis Carroll's *Sylvia and Bruno* (1889): 'He thought he saw a Banker's Clerk/Descending from the bus: He looked again and found it was/A Hippopotamus.'

savannas Tropical plain in America.

miasmal Fumes rising from malarial swamps.

Whispers of Immortality

Once more, in this poem written about 1918, Eliot returns to his favourite period, the seventeenth century, drawing upon John Webster (1580–1625) and John Donne (1572–1631) the metaphysical poet who was also Dean of St Paul's Cathedral. Their speculative mentality, concerned with problems of Non-Being in contrast to Being, dwelt much on death as the polar opposite of

sexual love, linked by the same axis. With Donne and the meta-
physical poets generally, according to Eliot's own essay on the
subject, intellect and sense coalesced.

The next section of the poem changes the scene to Grishkin's
maisonette. She gives promise of 'pneumatic bliss' – two words
much used in this context by Aldous Huxley in his *Brave New World*
(1932) and derived from the idea of air cushions.

Whispers of Immortality The poem's title is a play on Wordsworth's
'Intimations of Immortality'.

Webster His play *The White Devil* 5,4,130 supplies the image of the
flowers growing through the skull. There are echoes, too, of another
metaphysical poet Andrew Marvell (1621–78) in 'To his Coy Mistress':
'The grave's a fine and private place/But none, I think, do there
embrace.' Lines from 'The Relic' pin down the Donne reference: 'When
my grave is broke up again/Some second guest to entertain/ – For
graves have learn'd that woman-head,/To be to more than one a bed –/
And he that digs it, spies/A bracelet of bright hair about the bone.'

expert beyond experience Eliot is saying that Donne had a sensitive
knowledge of many things he had not personally experienced. This, of
course, is generally true of creative people, who can also seem to be
uncannily prophetic.

marmoset A small mammal, clearly alerted by the rank scent of the
predatory jaguar in the Brazilian jungle. The 'Abstract Entities' pacing
around Grishkin, drawn by her charm, have been compared with the
characters that prowl round Carmen in the novel of that name by
Prosper Mérimée (1803–70) – and on which Georges Bizet (1838–75)
based his famous opera.

our lot crawls ... metaphysics warm The last two lines of the poem
express the speaker's basic fear of contact with the flesh.

Mr Eliot's Sunday Morning Service

The first verse refers to the bees outside the window (returned to
in the seventh stanza); the 'sapient sutlers' are also priests.

The verses next turn to the first line of St John's gospel, then
allude to the doctrines of the early Church. Father Origen held
heretical beliefs about the Second Person of the Trinity, seeing him
as a copy of the Father, and thus inferior. Origen rejected the flesh,
and castrated himself.

This presentation of a false interpretation of the doctrine of God
the Son as the Word is followed by the description of a pre-

Raphaelite painting of the Baptism of Christ from the Italian school working in the province of Umbria, where Jesus Christ is shown in all his goodness, acclaimed by the Father and the Holy Spirit, *Paraclete* (Gr: 'Comforter').

Adolescents who have been brought to Church for the service, which begins with the confession of sin, are shown as spotty and clutching pennies for the collection.

There seems to be a reference to a rood screen before the sanctuary of the Church, with its opening, which is upheld by angels – here belonging to the highest angelic order, the Seraphim. There is an ironical allusion to those beyond the gates in the reference to a passage from Henry Vaughan's 17th-century poem 'Night': 'O for that night! Where I in him Might live invisible and dim.' Using an image from Jules Laforgue's poem 'Ballade', '*Une chair bêtement staminifère,/Un coeur illusoirement pistillé*', Eliot likens the clerics to the neuter worker-bees who pollinate plants, passing between the 'staminate' ('*staminifère*') flowers with stamens (male fertilizing organs) and the 'pistillate' ('*pistillé*': with pistils – female organs).

The hairy legs of the bees correspond to those of Eliot's character Sweeney, who is shifting his (hairy, as we already know) legs in his Sunday morning bath, just as the super-subtle theologians are continually shifting their doctrinal positions.

Look ... two religious caterpillars The epigraph is a quotation from *The Jew of Malta* by Christopher Marlowe (1564–93). The Jew Barabas and his servant Ithamore have just poisoned a whole convent of nuns and are poking fun at clerical figures, here two friars, whom they know to be unscrupulous and sexually immoral. Not only are they fond of fathering children, they do so with many different partners – they are 'polyphiloprogenitive'.

sapient Thinking.

sutlers Camp-followers; persons performing menial duties. Here subtle theologians are probably meant.

superfetation Over-fertilization.

τὸ ἕν (Gr.) 'The One'.

mensual Monthly.

enervate Languid; here, impotent.

presbyters Priests, Ministers of religion.

piaculative pence Pennies given in expiation of (atonement for) their – possibly fleshly – sins. The adverb 'piacular' means 'expiatory', from the Latin *piaculum*: 'expiation, atonement'.

epicene One who shares the characteristics of both sexes.
polymath Master of a wide range of knowledge.

Sweeney Among the Nightingales

The raven is a harbinger of death, especially in Norse literature. The constellation of Orion, the hunter and his hound, is also ominous, for Orion died through lechery. It appears that Sweeney is in danger from two women in a low 'dive'. A sinister man in brown is hanging about, observing from a distance. The story of Philomel – transformed into a nightingale – and her husband King Tereus, in Ovid's *Metamorphoses* is also based on adultery.

The sacrifice of the cross is recalled, the shedding of Christ's blood, through the mention of the Convent of the Sacred Heart, and linked with the story of Agamemnon's death. The connection with the nightingales in the 'bloody wood' of Sophocles enables Eliot, as George Williamson points out, by means of the 'liquid siftings', to cause song to pass, to stain.

Sweeney ... Nightingales There may be some relevance in the title to the legend of the Irish King, Sweeney, who was transformed into a bird. But of course 'Nightingale' is also a slang term for night-walkers, street walkers, figures from the underworld. There may also be some relevance in the suggestion of his friend Conrad Aiken, that Eliot's Sweeney was based, among other sources, on a prize-fighter of his acquaintance called Steve O'Donnell. The reference to the Nightingales comes from a tragedy by another ancient Greek dramatist Sophocles (*c*.496–*c*.405 BC), in his *Oedipus Coloneus* ('*Oedipus at Colonus*'). The title is also an echo of Browning's 'Bianca Among the Nightingales'.
maculate Spotted.
horned gate The gate of horn through which, in classical literature, dreams emerge.
mocha A drink made of combined chocolate and coffee. The flavour is richer than that of either drink alone; Eliot's use of 'mocha brown' thus suggests a rich brown.

Prufrock and Other Observations 1917

This collection of poems is dedicated to Eliot's close French friend, Jean Verdenal, who fell during the assault on the straits of the

Dardanelles, where the allied forces launched an attack on the Turks during World War I. He had shown Verdenal the poems before publishing them. During the time of writing, Eliot was reading Dante and Cavalcanti among Italian poets, Donne and the metaphysicals from the English seventeenth century, and the later French symbolist poets like Jules Laforgue and Baudelaire. The influence of all these writers can plainly be seen in the collection.

The Love Song of J. Alfred Prufrock

First published in Harriet Munroe's *Poetry*, Grover Smith mentions the suggestion that Henry James's story 'Grapy Cornelia' could have given Eliot the plot of the song. A middle-aged bachelor tentatively considers proposing to a young widow but draws back. Like Dante's Guido (see note below), Prufrock is in a hell of his own, but his fault has been frittering away his mental powers rather than actual destructiveness. He is in Hamlet's situation, but is behaving more like Polonius; he sees himself as 'an attendant lord'.

This whole sequence of poems reflects a preoccupation with the French symbolist poet Jules Laforgue's fascination with the figure of Hamlet, the tormented intellectual observer hesitating to commit himself.

Prufrock The name is taken from that of a leading family from the town of St Louis where Eliot grew up, as Stephen Stepancher has pointed out in 'The Origins of J. Alfred Prufrock' (*Modern Language Notes* 66).

S'io credessi ... ti rispondo The words of the epigraph are taken from the *Inferno*, Canto 27, where Guido da Montefeltrano, guilty of duplicity, confides in Dante from the eighth circle of Hell: 'If I thought my answer were to one whoever could return to the world, this flame should shake no more; but since none ever did return alive from this depth, if what I hear be true, without fear of infamy I answer thee.'

Michelangelo (1475–1564); great Italian Renaissance painter and sculptor from Florence whose most famous work was the painting of the vaulting of the Sistine Chapel in Rome.

there will be time ... for you ... for me These lines recall those of Andrew Marvell (1621–78) in 'To His Coy Mistress': 'Had we but world enough and time ...' This whole section of Eliot's poem, with its reiteration of the word 'time', also echoes Ecclesiastes, 3,1–8, which begins, 'To every thing there is a season, and a time to every purpose under the heaven ...'

When I am pinned Carries overtones of pinned-down specimens of butterflies and other insects – also of the French symbolist poet Jules Laforgue's poem 'Complaintes sur certains temps déplacés' and his 'Derniers Vers'; and of Baudelaire's 'Harmonies du soir' from *Les fleurs du mal.*

Arms braceleted ... light brown hair Echoes of John Donne's 'The Relic': 'A bracelet of bright hair about the bone'.

brought in upon a platter (See Matthew, 14,10,11: 'And he sent and beheaded John in the prison. And his head was brought in a charger.'

squeezed the universe into a ball Again the image comes from Marvell's 'To His Coy Mistress': 'Let us roll all our strength and all/Our sweetness up into one ball.'

I am Lazarus See John, Chapter 11. This comparison was suggested to Eliot by the *Crime and Punishment* of Feodor Dostoevsky (1821–81).

I have seen ... chambers of the sea There seems here to be an echo of John Masefield's poem 'Cardigan Bay' from his *Salt Water Ballads* (1902).

ragged claws ... floors of silent seas An evocation of self-hate, self-loathing: the self is being compared to primitive life.

Portrait of a Lady

The poem is, according to his friend Conrad Aiken, based on Eliot's friendship with an older woman – an enthusiast for culture – while he was at Cambridge, Massachusetts. By arousing a desperate attachment to him on the part of the elderly lady, disguised by a mutual interest in music, while he is largely indifferent to her, the young man commits a kind of outrage equivalent to the fornication referred to in Marlowe's play. He becomes embarrassed and tries to break off the relationship, making a foreign tour the excuse. But he departs feeling very uncomfortable about his own behaviour.

Portrait of a Lady The title is an obvious reference to Henry James's novel of that name, written in 1881. There are also possible echoes in the poem of James's *The Ambassadors* (1903).

Thou hast committed ... dead The epigraph is from Christopher Marlowe's *The Jew of Malta* 4,1.

Juliet's tomb To describe the atmosphere in her apartment the parallel of Juliet's tomb from the dénouement of Shakespeare's *Romeo and Juliet* is used.

cauchemar Nightmare; this use of the French word points up the lady's affections.

ariettes Brief musical airs.

My buried life, and Paris in the Spring A reference to a poem by Matthew Arnold (1822–88): 'A Buried Life'.

Achilles' heel Taken from the episode in the *Iliad* when Achilles's mother, the goddess Thetis, dipped him in the river Styx to make him proof against wounding. But she forgot that the heel by which she held him had not been touched by the river, so that it was in the heel that the Prince Paris was able to shoot the arrow which killed him.

My smile falls heavily ... bric-à-brac A telling metaphor: it sums up the whole embarrassing situation in which the young poet finds himself. ('Bric-à-brac': decorative bits and pieces.)

a dying fall See Duke Orsini's opening speech in Shakespeare's *Twelfth Night*, I,1,1–4.

Preludes

The title is from the musical form, the prelude (an introductory piece of music preceding a fugue or forming the first of a suite). The four poems, composed at different times (two at Harvard, the third in Paris and the last when Eliot came back to Harvard), introduce a street scene viewed at different times of the day and night. The woman in the third Prelude is a prostitute – drawn from Charles Louis Philippe's novel *Bubu de Montparnasse*. (Eliot's preface introduces the 1932 English translation of the book.)

The character in the fourth Prelude is the personified street itself. The idea of treating the street in this way probably derived from Philippe's *Marie Donadieu*, where Marie too has '... such a vision of the street/As the street hardly knows'.

Eliot's reading of Henri Bergson, the French philosopher (1859–1941), seems to have coloured all his poetry of this period, especially Bergson's treatment of matter and image in his *Matter and Memory*.

Rhapsody on a Windy Night

The title of this poem, written in 1915, is again based on a musical mode described as 'enthusiastic but of indefinite form'; the action is once more drawn from *Bubu de Montparnasse*, with imagery and atmosphere from Jules Laforgue's preoccupation with the moon and geraniums and with a detached self-regard.

Again Bergson's theories on the association of images and on memory play a part. Tricks are played with time, and from a vaguely sordid romanticism the speaker is brought back to the everyday realities of his lodging house: 'The last twist of the knife.'

fatalistic drum   See Oscar Wilde's *Ballad of Reading Gaol* (1898): 'But each man's heart beat thick and quick/Like a madman on a drum.'

The Waste Land

This poem was written mainly in 1921 while Eliot, who had been suffering from nervous strain, was recuperating in Switzerland, in the care of Dr Vittez of Lausanne, from November until the end of the year. On the way back through Paris he handed over the MS to his friend Ezra Pound, who set to work editing it immediately, and wrote to the Irish-American patron of modern letters, John Quinn, suggesting that the poem would shortly come out in the periodical *Dial* under Thayer.

Eliot has come back from his Lausanne specialist looking O.K.: and with a damn good poem (19 pages) in his suitcase; some finished up here; and should be out in *Dial* soon, if Thayer isn't utterly nutty.

Pound cut the poems very drastically, especially the 'Death by Water' section and, as Mrs Valerie Eliot, the poet's second wife, explains in her edition of *The Waste Land*, the poem was published 'almost simultaneously (ca. 15 October) in the *Criterion* and the *Dial*'. The first edition (with notes) appeared on 15 December [1922].

In gratitude for Quinn's help over negotiations for publication, Eliot gave him the original manuscript. After Quinn's death in 1924, the manuscript passed into the hands of his sister Mrs Anderson, and after her death was put into store. In the early 1950s Mrs Anderson's daughter, Mrs Conroy, found the manuscript and sold it to the Berg collection of the New York Public Library. It was not until 1968 that Mrs Eliot was able to obtain a microfilm of the manuscript from which to produce her edition, in which the original manuscript and the published first edition are compared, with notes and introduction.

Writing in his work on *The 'Pensées' of Pascal* (1931), Eliot describes his own composition of *The Waste Land* at Lausanne by explaining:

... it is a commonplace that some forms of illness are extremely favourable, not only to religious illumination, but to artistic and literary composition. A piece of writing meditated apparently without progress for months or years, may suddenly take shape and word; and in this state long passages may be produced which require little or no re-touch.

The manuscript of *The Waste Land* is, in fact, heavily corrected. But the poem did seem to flood out of his mind in the way he describes in this passage.

The major influence on *The Waste Land* comes from Jessie Weston's *From Ritual to Romance*, 1920 (see Eliot's 'Notes on *The Waste Land*, p.68, Faber paperback), though Eliot had probably been reading her *Quest of the Holy Grail* earlier. She sees the Grail story as a lightly Christianized version of the sacred banquet concept and the process of death followed by resurrection found in some of the Middle Eastern mystery cults; particularly that of Attis and Mithra, with very strong Gnostic overtones, which had been carried to Britain by the Roman legions and coalesced with native or vegetation myths. She pinpoints the author of the original Grail legend as one Bledri ap Cadivor, a Welsh nobleman from Dyfed. Thus a wounded, or maimed, or very old king, connected with the fish symbol – the pagan life-symbol as well as a Christian one – has to be rescued by a knight who passes certain tests, and who, above all, suffers an ordeal in the Chapel Perilous. He may be challenged also by a 'loathly lady', a hag, who later turns into a beautiful young girl, or he may be beguiled by a young woman who tries to seduce him. If he succeeds in his quest the king is healed, and with him the whole land returns from drought and sterility back to fertility and fruitfulness. The Quest is associated with the symbol of the Dove.

Since Eliot uses Hindu and Buddhist material that he had studied at Harvard University, much Greek classical material and Norse legends, and the symbolism of the Tarot Cards too, as well as Christian references, this all-embracing myth with somewhat sinister magical overtones suited his purposes very well. But he was directing his satire against godless modern city-life in general, and to some extent his own sense of *accidie* or paralysed depression in particular. His fascination with Elizabethan lyrics, Metaphysical poetry and Jacobean drama, which he had been teaching in Extra-Mural classes, is clear also, as is his attraction to Stravinsky's ballet music and Wagner's opera. The French symbolist poets had in-

fluenced him during his earlier stay in Paris, and the poems bear
the marks of the Surrealist movement that had affected all the Arts
on the Continent – and of course the marks, too, of his friend Ezra
Pound's editorial taste.

The Waste Land

Eliot has chosen the Greek mythological prophet Tiresias as the
figure who experiences the various episodes of *The Waste Land* and
passes through its labyrinth. This is because of Tiresias's crucial
role in such classics as the tragedy *Oedipus Rex* of Sophocles, and
in Homer; also because Tiresias, according to the myth, had
changed sex and so could understand the experience of life from
both a masculine and a feminine viewpoint. Here Tiresias's role
is mainly that of an observer in the background.

As in all of Eliot's poetry, many sources are referred to here.
In addition to Greek mythology (Tiresias) the principal sources for
The Waste Land are: the Bible (Old and New Testaments); the Grail
legend; Dante; Shakespeare; and above all the Tarot pack of
fortune-telling cards. Jessie Weston in *From Ritual to Romance*, recalls
that the suits in Tarot packs – cups, lances, swords and dishes –
use images that figure in the Grail legend. She also maintains that
the picture cards were used for predicting the rise and fall of the
Nile and the drying of the Chinese flood-waters. As Helen Williams
points out in her *T. S. Eliot: The Waste Land* (1973), Jessie Weston
also claims the origin of the words used in the pack as Sanskrit.
Helen Williams gives a useful summary of the Grail Legend itself:

the Fisher King has lost his virility through sexual mutilation or sickness
and this is associated with the desolation of his lands. Crops cannot grow
and the power of propagation is suspended. The curse of aridity can be
removed by a quester, a youthful knight who must undertake the journey
to the castle or chapel of the Grail, submit to trial, ascertain the office
of the Grail and the significance of the symbols of lance and cup. [In
fact, the lance which pierced Christ's side and the cup or chalice used
at the Last Supper and preserved by Joseph of Arimathea to receive some
of Christ's blook at the crucifixion.] If he succeeds the King will be healed
and the land restored to fertility.

Although Tiresias is the link figure throughout the poem, there are points when the author presents a more youthful quester figure in the forefront of the action, and Prince Ferdinand may be taking this part here, as at times even Phlebas the Phoenician sailor seems to. The counterpart of the quester is the Grail-bearer who is traditionally, Helen Williams explains, 'supposed to divine the quester and probe into the causes of his failure'. And as Grover Smith points out:

In certain versions of the myth the young Grail-bearer becomes an old witchwoman after the quester fails in his test. Old or young, the Grail-bearer is not generally of her own accord hostile to the quester, whose success can restore her beauty as well as the King's virility. Madame Sosostris may here be the witchwoman. When in *The Waste Land* the quester fails, she (occupying the sibyl's place in the initiation pattern), falls victim to a general desolation.

Grover Smith goes on to say that '. . . Belladonna, the Lady of the Rocks, the Lady of situations, who is clearly connected with the "drowned Phoenician Sailor", has been identified in the Tarot pack with the card of the Empress.'

'The man with three staves' has been associated with Osiris the Egyptian god, the type of the dying god resurrected. This picture-card, belonging to the Minor Arcana of the Tarot pack, is the three of Staves; Eliot, in his 'Notes on *The Waste Land*' (p.69), says that he associates this card 'quite arbitrarily, with the Fisher King himself'.

What has to be understood is that all these images refer to a draw of Tarot Cards and they represent the key symbols of the poem. Just as the first card which is laid out is personal to the subject of the fortune-telling so the last card in the draw is traditionally the more cosmic, impersonal one in its significance. It is natural that it should lead on into the 'Unreal City' sequence that follows the divination by the Tarot pack. Once she has finished with one customer Madame Sosostris thinks of her next. George Williamson suggests that 'dear Mrs Equitone' whose horoscope she is so concerned with may be the lady in Part 2 where 'nerves are bad tonight'.

The epigraph uses an allusion to the Sibyl of Cumae, or guardian of the gate to the underworld who uttered oracles from her shrine at the cavern of Cumae, taken from the *Satyricon* of Petronius. In D. G. Rossetti's translation:

I saw the Sibyl at Cumae
(One said) with mine own eye.
She hung in a cage, and read her rune
To all the passers-by.
Said the boys, 'what wouldst thou Sibyl?'
She answered, 'I would die.'

Grover Smith points out that the myth of the descent into Hell through a cave, as by Aeneas, was used by the Greek mystery cults for the initiation ordeals of their novices. The path to wisdom was seen as passing through a labyrinth.

The dedication to Ezra Pound, *'il miglior fabbro'* – 'the better craftsman' – (Dante, *The Divine Comedy, Purgatorio* 26,117), pays tribute to Pound's work as editor of the poem. The extent of Pound's work is revealed in Valerie Eliot's edition of *The Waste Land* (Faber & Faber, 1971).

Part 1   The Burial of the Dead

Throughout this section there are overtones from the traditional *Book of Common Prayer* service for the burial of the dead, with its texts from St Paul insisting that 'The dead shall be raised incorruptible, and we shall be changed.' This conviction is run together with the 19th-century poet James Thompson's concept of Mother Earth, in his poem 'To Our Ladies of Death' in *The City of Dreadful Night:* 'Our Mother feedeth thus our little life,/That we in turn may feed her with our death.' The sense of the seasonal struggle of new life out of the dead of winter is likewise fused with the poignancy of the hero Tiresias's memories.

Eliot's hero (brought forward into the twentieth century) first remembers the confidences given to him on her childhood adventures by a Lithuanian girl as he wanders with her into the Hofgarten park in Munich by the Starnberger-See. The picture of the Waste Land itself follows: the sterile rubbish of modern city life with overtones of the desert through which the children of Israel wandered (in the book of Exodus). The rock in this desert recalls that from which Moses struck water. But there is no water here: the only refuge is in the shadow of the rock – associated, among other things, with the rock of Peter, the foundation of the Christian Church. The experience that takes place in the shadow of the rock is at once inspiring and disappointing, like that of the Fisher King in the Grail legend, whose wound causes not only his own impotence but also the sterility of his land. (Eliot's major sources here are *The Quest of the Holy Grail* (1913) and *From Ritual to Romance* (1920), both by Jessie Weston.)

There is a failure to respond to the exhilarating moment of love with the 'hyacinth girl'. Then, contrasting with the fresh natural image of the hyacinth girl, who plays the role of the Grail Bearer, comes the fortune-teller Madame Sosostris.

Bin gar keine Russin ... echt deutsch The Lithuanian girl is saying (in German) that she is not Russian, is pure German. (This is 'lifted' from the Countess Marie's *My Past*.)

Frisch weht der Wind ... Wo weilest du The meaning of this German verse (from Wagner's *Tristan and Isolde*: see Eliot's note, p.68 Faber edition) is : 'The wind blows fresh/To the homeland/My Irish girl (lit. 'child')/Why do you tarry?'

You gave me hyacinths Again a mention of Eliot's favourite flower.

Oed' und leer das Meer Another line from *Tristan and Isolde* (see Eliot's note, p.68, Faber ed.): 'The sea is desolate and empty.' (*Note*: the German *Oede* means 'waste-land'.)

Madame Sosostris Her name was suggested by Aldous Huxley's novel *Chrome Yellow* (1921), where Mr Scogan disguises himself as 'Secostris, the Sorceress of Ecbatana', it stresses the idea of the female impersonator already conveyed by the use of Tiresias, through the fact that 'Sesostris' is actually the name of a 12th-century Egyptian king mentioned by the historian Herodotus. Madame Sosostris uses a pack of Tarot cards, the fortune-teller's stock-in-trade. The origins of the Tarot are mysterious. The cards have always been associated with Gypsy fortune-tellers and may have come to Europe with the Gypsy migrations from India, perhaps picking up influences from Persia and Egypt on the way.

Those are pearls ... eyes From Ariel's song in *The Tempest* about the supposed-drowned King of Naples.

Belladonna, the Lady of the Rocks ... of situations *Belladonna* is the Italian word for 'beautiful woman'; the 'Rocks' and 'situations' carry sinister overtones.

hypocrite lecteur ... semblable ... frère Here Eliot is addressing the 'hypocrite reader – my fellow ('resembler') – my brother!' In his notes at the end of *The Waste Land*, (see p.69), Eliot refers us to Baudelaire's preface to *Fleurs du Mal*, entitled 'Au lecteur' ('To the reader').

Part 2 A Game of Chess

The Belladonna figure, 'lady of situations' is seated on a 'Chair ... like a burnished throne' in this sequence; there are associations with passages describing Imogen's chamber in Shakespeare's *Cymbeline*, II,4,87–91, and Cleopatra's ceremonial encounter with Antony at Cydnus (*Antony and Cleopatra*, II,2,180). Dido, from Virgil's *Aeneid*, Book 1, line 725 (another queen, this time from Carthage), is also involved through Eliot's reference to perfumes (lines 87–9). Dido's burning on her funeral pyre is hinted at by the image of the cupola ('laquearia'), which reflects the flickering of the exotic green and orange flames, suffused with perfume and incense, that give an unearthly atmosphere to this vaguely occult scene. Its sinister nature is further emphasized by the representation of the story of Philomel above the mantlepiece. Philomel by the Elizabethan age had given her name to the nightingale because in the classical myth she was finally transformed into one by the Gods – in some versions into a swallow – hence the refrain 'Jug Jug', from 'Spring' by Thomas Nashe (1567–1601), also in lyrics by the dramatist John Lyly (1554?–1606).

The lady's plaints to her husband follow, alternating with his unsatisfying replies, which concern rats' alley with its dead men's bones. The wind she complains of he mentally associates with John Webster's 'Is the wind in that door since?' (*The Devil's Law Case*, 3,2). The couple's plans to divert their boredom next day include a game of chess while 'waiting for a knock on the door'. (Is there a suggestion of something shady, something connected with the underworld, perhaps – or with secret societies and dabbling in the Occult – in the situation of this couple? Or are they simply examples of sophisticates living loveless and pointless lives?)

The scene then changes to a pub (and a different social class), where Lil's relationship 'Now Albert's coming back' is being discussed; 'make yourself a bit smart' ... 'he wants a good time'. It transpires according to Lou, May and Bill, that Lil has taken pills to procure an abortion, which has not improved her health or her looks. The gossip is interrupted by calls from the landlord, about to close the pub: 'Hurry Up Please Its Time', which reminded the company and the reader, that 'it is later than you think'.

There is, throughout, the implied contrast between the fertility which the presence of the Grail should safeguard (especially when the chalice itself is associated with 'the food-producing cauldrons of Celtic Mythology', as Grover Smith remarks), and the sterility – and at the same time, lust – involved in Lil's story. (Perhaps the hot Sunday dinner of gammon at Albert's home is meant to suggest the feasting which often figures in the Grail Legend too, as well as to connect with the magic cauldron.) Thus, in Part 2, the drifting pointlessness and perversity of both upper- and lower-class life in the 'Waste Land' which Eliot is mapping out, is dramatized, underlining the quester's failure.

A Game of Chess The title is taken from that of a play by Thomas Middleton (1570?–1627), who also wrote the tragedy *Women Beware Women*, a play more relevant to this section of *The Waste Land*. In his note to line 137 (Faber edition p.81) Eliot explains that the game of chess is taken from *Women Beware Women*, where the Duke's seduction of Bianca (Act 2, Scene 2) is carried out while her mother-in-law's attention is distracted by a game of chess. (Williamson considers that this game, with its echoes from Middleton's play, is 'a cover for seduction, especially for "the lady of situations" in the upper class'. And Northrop Frye notes that Ferdinand and Miranda are discovered playing chess in *The Tempest*, V,1.)

sevenbranched candelabra This is reminiscent of the Jewish 'Menoreh', which stood in the Temple, and is still used in synagogues.

'Jug Jug' to dirty ears Appropriately, 'Jug, Jug' is sung to dirty ears, because the story itself (taken by Eliot, according to his notes, from Ovid's *Metamorphoses* 6) is so violent and degraded. King Tereus has raped his sister-in-law and cut out her tongue so that she cannot relate this to his wife. However she weaves a picture of the incident into tapestry and then, bent on revenge, the two sisters serve him a meal composed of the body of his own son. On their flight from Tereus the sisters are changed into birds: a swallow and a nightingale.

her hair ... fiery points There is a suggestion in this image of the Medusa, the Gorgon monster of Greek myth – originally a disgraced priestess – whose 'hair' consisted of snakes and whose gaze turned to stone anyone who looked upon her.

O O O O ... Shakespeherian Rag ... so intelligent The jazz rhythms of ragtime are represented in this sophisticated snatch; yet the 'O O O O' reminds us of the exlamations of King Lear (*King Lear*, III,2,24) and Othello (*Othello*, V,2,196).

Goodnight, ladies The final refrain carries echoes from a popular ballad 'Merrily we roll along', and from Ophelia's mad scene in *Hamlet*, IV,5.

Part 3 The Fire Sermon

The scene now shifts back to the Grail quester, standing at the waterside, only too conscious of his failure. These waters can be seen as Tristan and Isolde's sea, as the waters of Babylon beside which the Hebrews sat down and wept (Psalm 137,1). Or as the 'Sweet Thames' of the wedding song 'The Prothalamium' by the Elizabethan poet Edmund Spenser (1552–99). Or, again, as the Lake of Geneva (called by the French 'Lac Leman') – beside which, like Byron, Eliot is composing his poem. The nymphs who have departed are in one way Spenser's fertility nymphs, who have certainly left the Waste Land. In another they are the girls who had been enjoying the River Thames with 'their friends, the loitering heirs of City directors' and who have now gone home. An echo follows from the 17th-century Metaphysical poet, Andrew Marvell's lyric, 'To His Coy Mistress': 'And ever and again I hear,/ Time's winged charriot hurrying near.'

This connects with a further vision of the maimed Fisher King, who once more recalls Ferdinand's words (The Tempest, I,2): 'Sitting on a bank/Weeping again the King my father's wreck,/ This music crept by me upon the waters.'

There are allusions to Sweeney, underworld hero of Eliot's own sequence of Sweeney poems, as he visits Mrs Porter. She, in her turn, figures in a ribald song popular with World War I soldiers and still circulating in Australia. 'Mr. Eugenides the Smyrna merchant' trades in currants, which have perhaps an indirect link with the wine cup of the Grail. He comes from the Middle East and so it is not surprising he has been given connections with the Tarot Pack by critics. Grover Smith mentions some characteristics which could make him play the part of the Tarot Fool, the Hanged Man or the Patriarch (or Pope). Smyrna, his original city, was in the news at the time.

The poem's focus then shifts from the merchant to the blind Tiresias and the scene between the typist and the small house-agent's clerk, which is presented as typical of the many attempts to arrive at excitement and glamour being launched in the 'unreal city' 'at the violet hour'. The section ends with St Augustine of Hippo's lament in *Confessions*, 3,1 (see also Amos, 4,11), for his lost chastity in Carthage, which was to him 'a cauldron of unholy loves', and from which he was plucked as 'a brand from the burning'.

The Fire Sermon The title of this section is the name of the Buddha's most famous sermon, which corresponds to the Christian Sermon on the Mount, and in which Buddha describes how souls who have not yet attained enlightenment burn in the fires of *Tanha* or craving, the cause of all suffering and frustration: 'The eye, O Bikkhus, [disciples] is burning, visible things are burning; ... With what fire is it burning? I declare unto you that it is burning with the fire of lust.'

bones ... rattled The reference here is to a sequence from the *Ulysses* of the Irish writer James Joyce (1882–1941), where Mr Bloom is on his way to Paddy Dignam's funeral in Dublin: 'Rattle his bones. Over the Stones. Only a pauper. Nobody owns.'

Mrs Porter ... soda water Robert Payne in his *Great God Pan* gives this version of the ribald song:

> The moon shines bright on Mrs Porter
> And on her daughter:
> She washes out her ... in soda water,
> And so she oughta,
> To keep it clean.

Et O ces voix d'enfants ... coupole 'And O those children's voices, singing in the dome.' This quotation connects back again with the Grail legend, since the story of Sir Percival ('Parsifal' in Wagner's version), who overcomes his temptation to lust, cures the wounded King, and reverences the Grail, shows him hearing the voices of children singing in the dome above. The line itself comes from the sonnet 'Parsifal' by the French poet Paul Verlaine (1844–96).

demotic French The ordinary (non-literary) French of the common people; Mr Eugenides would speak a Levantine version of this.

The violet hour i.e. early evening. (Again Eliot introduces his favourite colour.)

carbuncular i.e. with boils and/or acne.

I Tiresias ... evening hour that strives Homeward Tiresias, the blind prophet figure who has 'foresuffered all' (line 243), perceives the scene in 'the evening hour that ... brings the sailor home from sea' – this last an echo from the 'Hesperus' of the Greek poetess Sappho (born *c.*650 BC); also from the poem 'Requiem' by the Scottish author Robert Louis Stevenson (1850–94). As Grover Smith remarks, there is a parallel in this episode with various accounts of attempted seduction of the quester by maidens, and of feasts spread out before him.

When lovely woman ... folly The typist's yielding is described in words from *The Vicar of Wakefield* by the playwright, novelist and poet Oliver Goldsmith (1728–74).

This music crept ... waters ... mandoline ... Magnus Martyr The music that 'crept by me upon the waters' is again a quotation from *The Tempest* (Act I, Scene 2) – Ferdinand's words when hearing the dirge. These strains melt into 'the whining of a mandoline' in a Thames-side pub, associated through its 'fishmen' clientele – from Billingsgate perhaps – with the Wren City Church of St Magnus Martyr; 'St Magnum and Pontem', originally erected in Fish Street and inevitably carrying connotations of the Fisher King.

Greenwich reach A section of the Thames; by Greenwich Palace, where Queen Elizabeth I of England (1533–1603) entertained her favourite, Robert, Earl of Leicester (*c*.1532–88).

Isle of Dogs Within a bend of the River Thames in East London. This reference may be intended to remind the reader of the alarming episode with a dog recounted by the waiter in Eliot's French poem 'Dans le Restaurant'.

Weialala ... leialala This is the lament of Wagner's Rhine Maidens – Woglinde, Wellgunde and Flosshilde – from his opera *Götterdämmerung* ('Twilight of the Gods'); they form a triad reminiscent in some ways of the Fates – each relates how she met her ruin.

Richmond and Kew ... Moorgate ... Margate Sands The first 'Thames daughter' is familiar with Richmond and Kew (favourite resorts of Elizabeth I); she met her downfall at Richmond. The second frequents Moorgate in the City; and the third – Grover Smith suggests the typist herself – is from Margate. (Because of their carnal weaknesses, Wagner's Rhine Maidens lose guardianship of the treasure entrusted to them, and only regain it from the pyre on which Brünnhilde has perished with Siegfried in the *Götterdämmerung*.)

Part 4 Death by Water

The draft for this section was originally eight pages long (including some repetition) before it was cut by Ezra Pound. In it Phlebas the Phoenician sailor who had figured in the battle of Mylae in the Punic War (and who is run together in some ways with Mr Eugenides the Syrian merchant and with Ferdinand of *The Tempest* too), is sucked down into a whirlpool – and there are perhaps punning overtones of Mr Eugenides's merchandise in the fact that a 'current ... picked his bones'. And Phlebas suffers the same death by water that was forewarned by Madame Sosostris. The actual disappearance into the whirlpool was suggested, according to Valerie Eliot, by Canto 26, 133–42, of Dante's *Inferno*, where Ulysses is encountered in Hell. Lines 316–18 'As he rose and fell ... entering the whirlpool'), and line 320 'O you who turn the wheel and look to windward') in their turn suggest not only the traditional idea of a man reviewing his whole life in the moment of drowning but the Buddhist concept of being bound to the wheel of birth and death. In the whole episode there is also an allusion to the rite described by the classic author Lucian and included in Jessie Weston's *From Ritual to Romance*, pp.44,48, by which a head of the God Adonis was cast into the sea at Alexandria every year and recovered seven days later by his devotees at Byblos where the current had swept it. The final appeal to those 'who turn the wheel and look to windward' is a 'memento mori' reminder: this drowned corpse 'was once handsome and tall as you'.

The whole of Part 4 is, of course, directly derivative of the last lines of Eliot's 'Dans le Restaurant' which, translated from the French, read:

Phlebas the Phoenician, drowned for fourteen days,
Forgot the gulls' cries and the billowing Cornish waves,
And the profits and losses, and the cargo of tin:
An undersea current carried him far away.
Taking him again through the stages of his earlier life,
Just think, what a horrible fate that was;
All the same, he was once a handsome man, and tall.

Part 5 What the Thunder Said

Having been planted in the earth and drowned at sea, the quester is now lost in the desert, away from garden or city and awaiting the Spring rains which the thunder over the mountains could presage. But there is no water and here, instead of yielding water as the rock did to Moses in the Sinai desert, there is only rock.

The destruction of civilization and the resultant migration of peoples are now mourned by composite voices of 'maternal lamentation'. It is appropriate that such destruction should figure at this point because the approach to the Chapel Perilous in the Grail Legend always poses great dangers. The woman's voices may be mourning for Christ; for the Syrian God Thammuz, slain like Adonis; or for Attis the consort of the Goddess Cybele who castrated himself and so is an image of sterility; or for Osiris the consort of Isis whose limbs were scattered wide. The falling cities may be 'Jerusalem Athens Alexandria Vienna London'.

By focusing on 'Falling Towers' Eliot draws attention to the Tarot Card of the Lightning-Struck Tower or 'Maison Dieu', number 16 of the Major Arcana. Arland Ussher's interpretation gives this as the 'falling Babel-Tower', which 'represents the necessary defeat of human action and conscious planning by the Incalculable Factor – a defeat supremely exemplified by the failure of the Crusades and the whole great moral and national synthesis of the Middle Age.' It perhaps points back to the original Fall, the fall of Lucifer, 'a destruction through intellectual more than sensual curiosity, as signified in the term "Le Maison Dieu".' There is a hint at the 'One-eyed merchant' again, since the Hebrew letter of the card is Ayin, the Eye, and its Zodiacal sign is Capricorn, symbol of discord, 'the Gate of the Gods' while 'in the individual life, disillusions and stresses have begun'.

At the last the scene shifts to the Fisher King speculating, 'shall I at last set my lands in order?' London Bridge and its downfall reintroduces the theme of the Falling Tower, perhaps the crumbling Grail Castle. There may be an allusion here, as Grover Smith notes, to the folklore belief in a blood sacrifice that must be built into the foundations of a bridge to ensure its stability.

The sound of the Sanskrit epilogue could convey the swish of falling rain upon *The Waste Land*, the breaking of the drought which the Fisher King has brought on his country. Or simply wish fulfilment, a mad delusion, depending on how optimistic or hopeless is the interpretation placed on this poem. An expression, in any case of a great poet's sense of the desolation of his own age.

After the torchlight ... is now dead   The first seven lines of this section obviously refer to Christ in the Garden of Gethsemane ('the agony in stony places'), his trial before Pilate, and his crucifixion on Golgotha.

Dead ... mouth ... cannot spit   This is derived from a legend in H. C. Warren's *Buddhism in Translation*. A monk achieves enlightenment through noticing the teeth of a woman who has opened her mouth to laugh at him when he begs alms. He realizes that he has been gazing at a collection of bones.

The third who walks ... beside you   A reference to Christ who, after his death, walked beside the disciples on the road to Emmaeus: they only recognized him from his gesture of breaking bread at the inn.

a man or a woman   The monk in H. C. Warren's translated legend (see note above) is asked by the dead woman's husband if he has seen her; he replies:

Was it a woman, or a man,
That passed this way? I cannot tell.
But this I know, a set of bones
Is travelling on upon this road.

(See also 'When Lilacs Last in the Door-yard Bloom'd' by the
American poet Walt Whitman, 1819–91): 'Then, with the knowledge of
death as walking on one side of me,/And the thought of death close
walking the other side of me . . .')

Falling towers . . . bats with baby faces . . . exhausted wells Eliot
himself explains that some of the 'falling tower' imagery (see lines
373–84) was inspired by the Renaissance artist Hieronymous Bosch's
panel *Hell*, forming a diptych with *The Deluge*, where, as Grover Smith
points out, 'there is a bat-like creature, with dull human features
crawling head first down a rock wall' – in a similar position to the
falling man before the tower on the Tarot card. As in the Mme
Sosostris sequence, there is a definite preoccupation in this section with
the sinister powers of magic. Grover Smith also suggests that the
shattered tower might signify the shell of organized religion which is
now crumbling, and to which the quester is turning at this stage.

cock . . . roof tree . . . co co rico The cock crowing inevitably recalls
the denial of Christ by his apostle Peter (Luke, Chapter 22): 'I tell thee,
Peter, the cock shall not crow this day, before that thou shalt deny
thrice that thou knowest me.' F. A. C. Wilson, in *Yeats and Tradition*,
pp.280–81, suggests another image: 'It is a reminiscence of a detail in the
ritual of the Golden Dawn in which the bird of Hermes . . . was
represented as perched at the summit of the Kabbalistic tree of life.'

DA/Datta . . . Dayadhvam . . . Damyata This is the voice of the
Thunder; the source is an Indian legend in one of the sacred
Upanishads. The meanings of the Sanskrit words are: *Datta* – 'give';
Dayadhvam – 'sympathize'; *Damyata* – 'control'.

Poi s'ascose . . . gli affina (It.): 'Then he dived back into the fire that
refines them.' This is a quotation from Dante's *Purgatorio*: Dante,
climbing the Mount of Purgatory, has been speaking with Arnaut
Daniel, who begs him to remember his (Arnaut's) pains, then dives
back into the 'cleansing fires of Purgatory'.

Quando . . . chelidon (L.) 'When shall I be like the swallow?' – another
version of the Philomel legend from the 'Pervigilium Veneris' ('The
Vigil of Venus') by an unknown Latin poet, where Philomel turns into
a swallow rather than a nightingale.

Le Prince d'Aquitaine à la tour abolie (Fr.): 'The Prince of
Aquitaine, of the ruined tower'; an allusion to the disinherited Prince of
the French sonnet by Gérard de Nerval (1808–55).

Hieronymo's mad againe A reference to the sub-title of *The Spanish
Tragedy*, written in blank verse by Thomas Kyd (1558?–94?), one of the
best-known tragedy writers of Elizabethan times. *The Spanish Tragedy* is
the story of the old man Hieronymo's vengeance for his son Horatio's
hanging. He uses for his own deadly purposes the arrangements for an
entertainment for the Viceroy; in his manipulation of the other

characters and his frantic utterances Hieronymo takes on the role of another Tiresias figure. His frenzy as he prepares his trap makes his hearers think him mad.

Shantih ... shantih This Sanskrit word (as Eliot explains in his Note on p.74, Faber edition) means 'The Peace that passeth understanding'. The Hebrew equivalent is 'Shalom'.

Questions

1 How many of Eliot's *Selected Poems* reveal an inability to love?

2 Consider Eliot's use of imagery in *Ash Wednesday*.

3 A woman drew her long black hair out tight
And fiddled whisper music on those strings
And bats with baby faces in the violet light
Whistled, and beat their wings
And crawled head downward down a blackened wall
And upside down in air were towers
Tolling reminiscent bells, that kept the hours
And voices singing out of empty cisterns and exhausted wells.

What is Eliot trying to convey by his passage in *The Waste Land*?

4 Give an appreciation of the pub scene in the 'Game of Chess' section of *The Waste Land*.

5 What kind of picture do we build up of J. Alfred Prufrock?

6 Comment on this expression from *Gerontion*: 'In the juvescence of the year/Came Christ the Tiger'.

7 Explain how Eliot creates atmosphere in 'Rhapsody on a Windy Night'.

8 Discuss Eliot's musical imagery.

9 What feeling comes through in 'Journey of the Magi'?

10 How is the sea used in 'Marina'?

11 In what way is Eliot's learning reflected in his poems?

12 Discuss *either* Eliot's use of the colloquial *or* his use of repetition in *Selected Poems*.